Cynthia Rylant

A Writer's Story

by Alice Cary

illustrated by Susan Spellman

Scott Foresman

Editorial Offices: Glenview, Illinois • New York, New York
Sales Offices: Reading, Massachusetts • Duluth, Georgia
Glenview, Illinois • Carrollton, Texas • Menlo Park, California

Cynthia Rylant loves to write.
She writes many kinds of books.
Picture books. Novels. Nonfiction.
Even poetry. Her books are in thousands
of libraries.

How does she work? How did she
become an author?

Cynthia was born in 1954. She grew
up in West Virginia.

As a girl, Cynthia did not have many
books. There were no libraries or museums
in her town. Not even a bookstore.

She read comic books. She read
about a girl named Nancy Drew. She
read a few fairy tales. That was
about all.

Cynthia lived in a small house with her grandmother and grandfather. They had to use an outdoor bathroom, or outhouse.

Cynthia didn't know she was poor. She felt rich.

She loved the mountains. She loved playing, walking, and thinking.

"I loved everything about life," she said.

As she got older, Rylant thought about being a teacher or a nurse, like her mother.

After college, she worked in a library. In the children's room, she found something new. Children's books!

She read them every night.

She loved two books best. One was called *The Animal Family*. The other was *The Ox-Cart Man*. She really admired the authors of these books.

She read these books over and over. She began to write her own stories.

6

When Rylant was twenty-five, she
sent one of her stories to a publisher.
Soon she learned it would become
a book.

"I'll never forget that day," she says.
When I Was Young in the Mountains
is about growing up in West Virginia.

Now Rylant was an author!

Rylant now lives in Oregon. She works quickly and quietly, like a mouse.

"I write on notebook paper when nobody is home," she says.

Sometimes she works on two projects. She might do a novel in the morning and a picture book after lunch.

But Rylant, like many other authors, doesn't write every day. Sometimes weeks or months go by without her writing anything.

Rylant writes about things she loves. The topics include family, friends, pets, and the mountains.

She watches for fun places. She listens for funny names.

"I bet there's a book there," Rylant may say. Then she turns that idea into a story.

People and animals may inspire
her. A man named Mr. Putter and a
dog named Zeke are in some of her
books. She also writes about a boy
named Henry and his dog Mudge.

She had a neighbor like Mr. Putter.
She knew dogs like Mudge and Zeke.

Once Rylant talked with a publisher.
He wished for a book about scarecrows.

Rylant went home and wrote a story
that day.

You can read that story in her book,
Scarecrow.

Rylant loves to try new things. One day she went to a store. She got scissors and paper. Then she made illustrations for a story.

"It was one of the most difficult things I've ever done," she says.

Although she finds it difficult, she has illustrated several books.

Rylant knows how to write a good book. She says that she starts with her imagination. Next she finds an interesting plot. And then she adds details.

"The things that make stories great are little details," she says.

How does imagination come?

"You have to sit quietly, clear your mind, and wait," she says.

"Most people can't get past the first part," she adds. "They can't sit quietly."

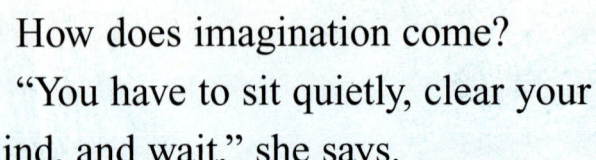

Rylant's books are famous. But she is not. She likes it that way.

She gives very few interviews. Once she won an important award. *The Today Show* wanted an interview. Rylant just said no.

Most people don't know she's a writer. Not even her neighbors.

In fact, Cynthia Rylant is not even her real name!

"I am a little timid in life," Rylant
says. "But I am brave in my work."
Her days are quiet and simple.
"That way I'm ready to sit down
and write when it's time," she explains.